A BEGINNERS GUIDE TO ARCHERY FORM

BY DAVID MULLEN

TABLE OF CONTENTS

INTRODUCTION

Developing proper archery form is as critical as having a well-tuned bow and the correct arrows. Even the best bow on the market will not perform with any great accuracy without proper form. There are many elements involved with archery form and as a beginner it can be quite frustrating at first but when practiced good archery form will become second nature to you.

Before attempting to master your form, it is important you have the right bow (hand, length and weight) and arrows (spine, shaft and length). If you are just starting out in archery and have not bought your equipment yet then I would recommend reading the first edition of this series *'A Beginners Guide to Recurve Archery Equipment'* which is also available on Amazon. You can practice your form without having a bow in front of you but be aware that the wrong equipment will equally affect your shooting accuracy as would poor form. You can have great equipment but poor accuracy due to your form and vice versa.

A Beginners Guide to Recurve Archery Equipment 8 Jun 2014
by David Mullen

Kindle Edition   ★★★★★ ▾ 12
£0.00 kindle unlimited   £1 AV Reward See Details
Read this and over 1 million books with Kindle Unlimited.

£0.99 to buy
Available for download now

Paperback
£9.95 ✓prime
In stock

Available on Kindle and Paperback

As a beginner, you may find yourself saying '*I did that shot the same as the last but the arrows are way off*'. This is quite common and is it worth remembering that archery is unforgiving and even the slightest of error can cause your arrows to wander off target. It takes a great deal of patience to perfect your archery form and it is important not to let the bad shots affect your confidence as even the experienced archers have a bad day. Practice makes perfect and if you practice your form at least three times a week to begin with you should notice a big difference in only a few weeks and the grouping of your arrows will improve.

It is worth practicing your form with others as you cannot see yourself from all angles when practicing your form and others can point out any errors to help you. Using a mirror at home can also help to make sure you have a good alignment but make sure you don't have an arrow loaded in your bow, you can purchase an exercise band relatively cheap that helps to practice form without having to put your bow up.

Always remember that archery is fun and try not to get too frustrated when practicing your form. You need to adopt a positive attitude as a negative one with affect your shots every time. Ease up and have fun, relax and get over bad shots quickly. It is also important to know your limits, do not practice for long periods as you will become both mentally and physically tired therefore practicing is useless. Take regular breaks between sessions to assess your progress and talk to others at the shooting range.

This book will guide you through the key parts of archery form; stance, grip, finger position, preparing the shot, drawing the bow, anchoring, aiming, loosing and follow through. It is a good place to start for beginners and for those wishing to improve their form and find consistency in finding the center of the target. At the end of this book is also a list of archery terms or jargon to assist beginners in finding their feet on the range.

CHAPTER ONE
THE BASICS FIRST

WARM UP!

It may appear obvious to most of us, however even experienced archers are guilty of forgetting to warm up before a shoot. A good warm up is critical to help prevent any injuries and can help you improve your consistency. It is a good idea to try different warm ups and exercises before shooting so you don't become bored and to flex different muscle groups. The best warm ups are stretching exercises only (not straining) and should be performed with a simple "hold and release" action. Below are a few simple warm ups to perform which ideally should follow a few minutes vigorous activity to get the heart rate pumping.

THE HUG

Wrap your arms around you and hold your right shoulder with you left hand and vice versa for around eight seconds each.

THE SHRUG

Raise your shoulders high and hold for two seconds then relax for four seconds. This should be repeated between 4-6 times.

ROTATING SHRUG

While relaxing your arms, rotate your shoulders in a circular motion, forwards then backwards, for around 8-10 repetitions.

HORIZONTAL SHOULDER STRETCH

With your left arm horizontal, bring your left palm over your right shoulder. With your right hand, pull the left elbow towards you and hold for eight seconds.

VERTICAL SHOULDER STRETCH

Raise your left arm up and place your left hand between your shoulder blades. With your right hand, pull your left elbow to the right and hold for eight seconds.

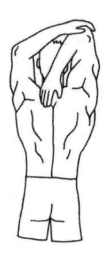

REAR ARM STRETCH

Place your left arm behind your back with the left arm at your right side. Clasp your left hand with your right hand and pull gently. Hold for eight seconds then repeat with the right arm.

THE VERTICAL ARM STRETCH

Clasp both hands and stretch arms upwards. Rotate hands until your palms face upwards. Push upwards and hold for eight seconds.

ARM CIRCLES

Hold both arms vertical and swing them in large circles, both in the same direction. Swing the left arm forward and right arm backwards then vice versa.

TRUNK TWISTS

Lift both arms out sideways and twist at the waist to the left, then to the right. Repeat 4-5 times.

NECK STRETCHING

Looking straight ahead, tilt head over to the left and hold for eight seconds. Repeat with your head tilted to the right. Hold for around eight seconds. "DO NOT OVERDOO NECK STRECHING" The neck muscles and nerves can be delicate therefore it is wise to only perform a few of these.

If this is your first time exercising for a while then it is always recommended to seek medical approval before starting exercises or a new sport.

PHYSICAL TRAINING

Training is important if you want to improve your form and will develop the muscles required to shoot consistently. Your club coach will have an appropriate set of exercises for you to follow and the following is a good guide to start from.

The Formaster

The Formaster is used in different exercises and is great to use when you cannot get to a range, at work during breaks or at home in from of the television.

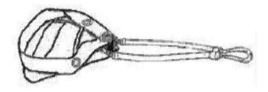

The first exercise with the Formaster is known as *"Reversals"*. Attach the Formaster to the string near the nocking point and using your ELBOW only, draw the bow to full draw and hold for 30 seconds. Release and relax for 30 seconds. For those who are new to this exercise, use a shorter holding time (10-20 seconds) and gradually build up as strength increases.

Repeat this exercise at least once or twice a week (preferably every day on which you do not shoot). After two to four weeks you should be able to repeat the 1-minute draw/relax cycle 10 times. Once you can do 20 repetitions of the 30-second cycle, you are beginning to get strong enough to control your bow effectively – at this stage, you might consider moving on to reversals using heavier limbs.

Once you have started your reversals, you may find it helps to flex the shoulder muscles in small, repetitive movements (i.e. pushing the bow shoulder out and down, and the drawing shoulder round and back.) to promote flexibility and movement as well as build strength in some of the smaller muscles.

"Back Tension" exercises are another workout with the Formaster which is good for promoting balance, working the back muscles, and teaching good bow arm follow through.

Stand close to a target butt and put a target pin in the butt to provide a point of reference. Attach the Formaster to the string just above the nocking point and nock an arrow. Draw the bow, sight the target pin and pull the arrow through the clicker, focusing on the aiming point. Release the arrow as normal. One of two things will happen:

- The drawing elbow will not move, or may move back slightly. This is good as it means that there was no premature relaxation after the shot, and that the back muscles were being used effectively.
- The drawing elbow will be pulled forward (collapse). This is bad as it means that the muscles were relaxed too early and there was therefore a poor follow through. It also indicates use of the wrong muscles for drawing.

Repeat 25 times or more to build muscle memory. This muscle memory lasts for some time, but will eventually fade and so must be reinforced. As time goes on, the muscle memory will last for longer and longer periods. Try to combine a routine of shots with and without the Formaster.

BOW EXERCISE WITHOUT SHOOTING

This exercise can be good for strength building, promoting clicker control and avoid pinching the arrow. Stand close to a target butt and put a target pin in the butt to provide a point of reference. Nock an arrow. Draw the bow, sight the target pin and pull the arrow through the clicker, focusing on the aiming point. Repeat as necessary.

Things to remember when performing this exercise:

- **DO NOT** let go of the arrow when the clicker goes off.
- Make sure that the sight ring stays near the sight point after the clicker has dropped
- Try to ensure you maintain tension when the clicker has dropped, and that the tension is directed at the aiming point
- Ensure the arrow does not drop off the rest either before, during or after the draw and release.

Repeat as above, but watch the clicker. Observe the smooth and progressive movement of the point under the clicker. Be aware of the motion of your arms/shoulders as you draw the arrow back smoothly.

MENTAL TRAINING

It is worth remembering that we all make bad shots, but we should also remember that we "HAVE" to make bad shots to work out how to make the good ones. Do not over analyze the bad shots as this creates negativity and will eventually take the enjoyment out of archery. It is more productive to analyze the good shots – how did I make this shot? Did I do anything different?

Mental imagery can also be helpful when you are not at the club or range. Picture the target in front of you and shooting the arrows into the ten ring, even make imaginary actions while picturing the target. Sometimes practice without the bow can be just as beneficial.

WHICH HAND TO SHOOT WITH?

The decision of which hand to shoot with appears to favor the eye-dominance theory. If you are right eye-dominant, then you should be a right-handed archer. So, how do you tell? Following the method below can help determine which hand to shoot with:

- Hold hands out at arm's length with both eyes open
- Look through a hole in your hands at a distant object
- Keeping the object in view, move hands towards your face until they touch your face
- The hole formed in your hands should be over one eye

This eye, in theory, should be your dominant eye and will control your aiming. Shooting with both eyes open can be an issue with aiming as you will see two sight rings and one target. It is better to shoot with your dominant eye open. In theory, if you are right handed you should shoot with your left eye closed or obscured and vice versa. If you cannot determine which eye is dominant, shoot with your left eye closed (for right-handed) and right eye closed (for left-handed).

CHAPTER TWO

STANCE

Stance is one of the most basic poses of an archer and is the foundation of the shot. A poor stance will result in a poor shot, particularly in windy conditions which will weaken a poor stance. Many changes come into being in the angles of the entire body which relate to the basic form of the stance. Some small changes may need to be introduced to be in accordance with an archer's physical shape of the body and the characteristics of the pose. However, it is most important for an archer to master an accurate and basic square stance when they are in the beginning stages. Once the archer moves on to the improving stage it is better for them to choose the stance that suits their body structure and them as an individual.

THE FEET

Foot placement during a shot can affect arrow flight. Your body has a natural centering point and if your feet are not positioned properly, your shot may be directed towards your centering point in a fraction of a second during the shot. There are three basic foot positions all of which should be shoulder's width apart.

Shoulder width

THE CENTER LINE

The center line of a body at the time of assuming the stance is very important. This center line of the body is under continuous movement while the bow is being drawn. Even at the time of extending the body to complete the shot a lot of influence is exerted and the line may deviate from the vertical. The archer should be particularly careful to maintain the vertical position. Right handed archers hold the bow with the left hand, so with your left side toward the target, stand at a right angle to the target, with the tips of your toes against an imaginary line pointing at the center of the target.

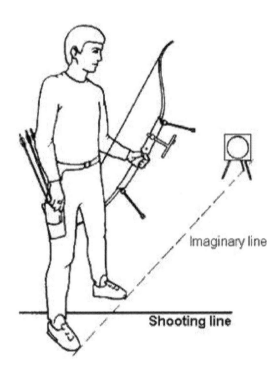

Imaginary line

Shooting line

THE SQUARE STANCE

The square stance is the best way to start off in archery because it is very easy to learn and simple enough to consistently reproduce. Rotate your feet into what we call the "square stance". The square stance means your feet are parallel to the shooting line. The square stance facilitates good biomechanical alignment by placing the hips and shoulders "in line" with your direction of aim or perpendicular to the target face. Learning the square stance first will produce fewer variations in your shot execution and *help you to realize tighter arrow groups and accuracy in a shorter time* resulting in less frustration during the learning period.

THE OPEN STANCE

The "open stance" is much more difficult to perfect and if it is not properly executed you will experience misalignment of the hips and shoulders and uneven weight distributions that make you unstable.

The open stance is ideal when a side wind is present, when there are issues with clearance on the bow arm or clothing. Although the feet are at an angle with the open stance, the upper body must be twisted above the waist to maintain the shot. The line of the shot is crucial throughout the shot and should be maintained until the arrow has hit the target.

When using the open stance, the width of the feet is to be in line with the shoulders. If the direction of the waist is on the same line as the feet, the position of the bow shoulder is pushed backward making it difficult to maintain the power at full draw. When the twisting of waist is too strong, the flexibility of the body comes to disappear and archers start to feel tension in the upper body. Also, movement takes place in the waist causing the bow shoulder and arm to shake making it impossible to produce a good shot. The open stance, if done correctly can have an advantage in which the archer can have a feeling of stability in windy conditions.

In the open stance, the front foot is towards the archer's backside, the back foot is aligned with the toes of the front foot. This provides a stable support base and prevents leaning away which can be a problem with the square stance.

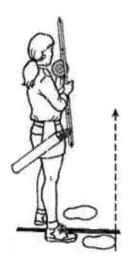

THE CLOSE STANCE

In this position, the front foot is forward from the front of the body such that the heel of the front foot is aligned with the toes of the back foot. The stance provides a stable support base and good alignment of the arm and shoulder with the target.

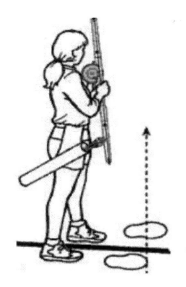

THE OBLIQUE STANCE

This last stance is like the open stance and is only slightly different. The archer places the big toe of their front foot on a line and pivots 45 degrees to the target. The heel of the back foot is placed in line with the big toe of the front foot. The stance provides the best amount of clearance for the bowstring when releasing the arrows. It also allows for better aim by seeing the target clearer than other stances. Although there are advantages to this stance, it is mainly used by the more experienced archer as it can be difficult to maintain.

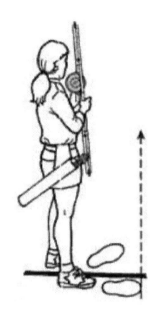

Below is a good checklist to keep in mind when taking your shots. Regular referral to the checklist will result in the process becoming automatic, improving your chance of good shooting.

- Stand tall and relaxed, one foot on each side of the shooting line
- Don't lock the knees
- Keep your feet shoulder width apart
- Keep an even balance on both feet
- Keep the same foot position for each shot (using markers can help)
- Keep your shoulders square and head level

If you are a beginner, the most common stances used are the square and open stance as they are easier to master and maintain to start with. It is not recommended that the other stances are attempted until you are at least competent with the square and open stances.

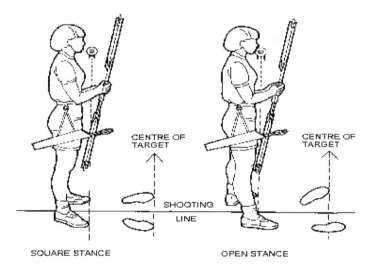

CHAPTER THREE

THE PRE-DRAW

This provides a good opportunity to get the basics right, establish a good grip of the bow and string, and relax before executing the shot. It is good practice to perform pre-draw activities without shooting as this will train your body and mind before target practice.

NOCK THE ARROW

Nocking the arrow is the process of holding the arrow so you can snap the nock onto the bowstring. Attach the arrow to the string by pushing the nock firmly onto the finger serving below and between the nocking points. Ensure the arrow is not too tight or too loose as this will affect the shot. To check this, hang the arrow vertically from the string and tap the string which should make the arrow drop off. If you have a clicker and/or pressure button fitted, ensure the arrow is resting against the pressure button and under the clicker.

The basic steps to knocking an arrow are as follows;

- Hold the arrow shaft close to the nock behind the arrows fletching/vanes.
- Place the arrow shaft on the rest.
- Rotate the shaft so the index vane is pointing outwards, away from the bow.
- Click the nock of the arrow onto the bowstring between the nock locaters (if used)
- **** KEEP THE ARROWS POINTED DOWN RANGE AT ALL TIMES WHILE NOCKING THE ARROWS ****

Over time, most archers develop their own method of nocking their arrows, however the above is a good starting point for beginners and those wishing to refresh from the beginner's course.

DRAWING HAND

This step relates to griping the bow and string correctly for optimum shooting. The index, second and third fingers are normally for gripping the string in target archery. The index finger is placed above the nock, and the second and third fingers are placed below the arrow nock.

Curl the fingers around the bowstring so that string is resting on or behind the first joint of all three fingers. Some archers believe that a deeper hook around the string can be more relaxing resulting in a cleaner release. However, it can feel like too much finger to move out of the way to release.

Keep a clear space between the index and second fingers and the arrow knock to prevent the fingers touching the nock (pinching the arrow). The result of pinching is that the arrow is drawn sideways off the rest as the string is drawn back, a way to prevent this is using a finger tab with a spacer which prevents pinching. Keep the back of the hand as flat as possible and tuck the thumb in so it is resting against your neck at full draw. An even pressure should be kept on each finger at beginner's level whereas more experienced archers may vary this.

BOW HAND

Place the bow hand into the grip of the bow with the centerline of the V-shape between thumb and index finger in line with the center of the bow as shown in the top view. The base of the thumb muscle should rest on the centerline of the grip. During the draw, the pressure should be taken on the thumb muscle and directly into the wrist.

The thumb and fingers should remain relaxed. If a finger sling or bow sling is not used, then the tips of the fingers are curled around until lightly touching the bow. This will stop the bow falling out of the hand on release. A consistent hand position on the bow grip is essential to consistent shooting.

Rotate the arm so that when the bow is lifted, the knuckles of the hand are at an angle of approximately 45 degrees. I have found that this is easier to do consistently if the three outer fingers are curled under and tucked in beside the riser.

There are three possible positions for the wrist;

High Grip - With a high grip the wrist is raised and in line with the knuckle of the index finger.
Medium and Low Grip - With the medium & low grip, the pressure is lowered to the fleshy part of the thumb.

BOW ARM AND DRAWING ARM

The bow arm is one of the most important parts of the shot, other than the release and follow through. It must be stable and strong and of consistent length from shot to shot. To achieve strength, the archer should aim to keep the shoulder aligned with the socket as much as possible, and this can be done by maintaining a slightly low shoulder. Raise the bow arm by rotating at the shoulder and check to see that the shoulder stays low.

Keeping the shoulder down will also stop it rising during the draw, and thereby shortening the draw and as a result moving the clicker out of reach. Keep the elbow of the drawing arm high – this will make it easier to correctly use the large back muscles, and therefore allow the drawing arm and hand to remain relaxed.

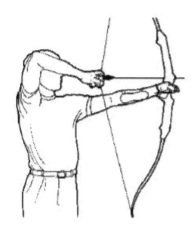

THE DRAW AND ANCHOR

Keep the front arm fully extended, but not over extended (there should be little or no room to "push" from the bow arm) as you draw in a smooth flowing motion in as direct a line as possible all the way back to the "anchor" position.

Draw the string straight back whilst maintaining a relaxed drawing arm – in this way, the arm will be moved by the powerful back muscles. Using the back muscles is an excellent way to develop consistency and stamina. Using the arm muscles will cause fatigue and result in an inconsistent release and follow through.

The elbow of the drawing arm should be in line, or slightly higher than the line of the arrow. Having "good line" makes the shot and follow-through much more consistent.

The "anchor" position is where the hand is positioned on the jaw and the bowstring touches the face and should provide a consistent point of reference. Some archers bring the string back to the center of the chin, others slightly to the side however, there are some do's and don'ts:

- **DO** lightly touch the tip of your nose with the string.
- **DON'T** bring the string beyond the square of your chin – this may result in the string hitting the chin on its way past.
- **DO** keep your hand close to your neck and remember to keep the back of your hand flat.
- **DO** place the index finger firmly under the jaw to develop a good solid reference point

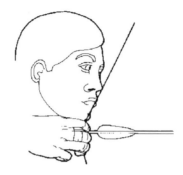

Some archers use "kisser buttons". Small pieces of plastic attached to the string which is placed against the lips, or a tooth. It is important, when using such a device, to ensure that the position on the face, wherever it is, is repeatable. Anchoring at the corner of your mouth is not recommended as this can move in all directions. Lightly placed between the lips is acceptable, provided your facial expression does not change too much.

When the string is in place, one final check is important, and that is "String Picture". This is crucial, especially at long distances. When looking through the sight, you will see a blurred image of the string, it is important that this is aligned to the same point for every shot. If it's slightly off, rotating your head slightly will correct this. If the string picture is in the wrong place, then your aiming accuracy will be off and the result will be groups which are spread horizontally. For alignment, many European archers use the side or center of the riser or sight-window, others use the side of the sight aperture, although this method can cause problems when the windage has to be adjusted.

When you get to anchor it is very important that you don't stop pulling. Changing from a "pulling" action to a "holding" action will make it very difficult to return to the pull, and so the arm muscles are likely to tighten up. This makes it more difficult to pull, and it becomes very difficult to get through the clicker.

Finally, the aiming of the arrow. There is no actual need to aim as we automatically do this subconsciously. Let the sight float around the gold. When the clicker goes off, and the release occurs, your brain will automatically center the sight on the gold, all you should do is set the shot up correctly, and let your subconscious take control.

THE RELEASE AND FOLLOW THROUGH

As mentioned earlier on, the release (or "loose") is another critical factor in any shot. A relaxed release and continuous follow through will make the difference between an average shot and a stunningly good shot. This is where the "feel" of the shot is all important. It is something we must learn through many hours of practice. We should learn to know what a good shot feels like, and then we begin to develop a rhythm and consistency.

Maintain the pulling movement. This takes commitment to the shot. When that bow is up, and the gold is in the sight-ring, either go for the shot wholeheartedly or come down. No half measure is good enough. If you're not committed to the shot then only luck will make it a good one.

But don't forget that solid front arm. Don't allow the front shoulder to rise, focus on the gold. Reach for the target whilst continuing the motion. Feel the balance between the front arm and the back arm. Note we say "reach" here, remember that the arm is locked, and the shoulder down so there is very little movement available. Simply strengthen the line, in the direction of the target.

As you continue to pull back the clicker will click. This is not the signal to panic, that kind of reaction will cause an uncontrolled or "explosive" release, resulting in an erratic, unpredictable shot. The clicker is the signal to allow the subconscious to let go, when it is ready, so simply relax and let the shot flow.

Some archers tend to look to see where the arrow is going but this is not good practice. Anything we do above and beyond shooting at the gold is a distraction. Once the arrow has gone, it is too late. Simply focus on making the perfect shot into the gold.

Focus is extremely important. Staying with the task at hand is difficult for humans. The average person has an attention span of approximately 2-3 seconds, so developing focus is a key feature for all successful archers. From the pre-draw to the follow-through we should be single-minded, aware of our body and the feel of the shot, but committed to the center of the target.

RYTHUM

Muscle memory is key to archery, and one of the best ways of developing muscle memory is shooting with a consistent rhythm in continuous motion, and repeating this process over again for as many arrows as you can realistically shoot. A good consistent rhythm will provide a strong consistency to the entire shot process. Developing rhythm and motion is best done without a target face. A technique which is generally regarded as extremely useful. Every archer should have a "rhythm" session at least once or twice a week.

Remove the sight-bar, stand close to a boss and simply shoot arrows. Don't think about the aim, simply ensure that each shot feels right, and shoot every arrow with focus and commitment. Try to develop a rhythm and try to maintain that rhythm for as many arrows as you can, concentrating on the feel. Concentrate on the form and enjoy the feeling of shooting just for the sake of it. This, more than anything, can develop consistency.

If you cannot make it to the range/club then you could buy a Formaster device. This device consists of an elbow cup with a cord which effectively attaches your elbow to the string. Using this device and a reasonably long hallway (or garden) you can practice pre-draw, draw, anchor and clicker control without risking damage to arrows or property. Simply draw through the clicker, hold for a few seconds and let the arrow down gently without letting go. Even if you let go, the Formaster should be set so that the arrow will do no damage and will not be damaged itself.

CHAPTER FOUR

COMMON PROBLEMS

Frustration

All archers experience the frustration of one day hitting perfect shots and the next hitting the dirt. What do you do? Keep struggling, with dogged determination? Give up? Worry? Get angry with yourself? The best way to tackle the frustration is to go back to basics.

Make a check list of your weaknesses, the points on which you feel you need to concentrate. Throw away the bad habits developed and go back to the beginning, start afresh. Start off slowly and you will soon be back shooting the way you know you can.

Target Panic

An eternal problem for archers of all disciplines, and one for which there are many causes and no easy solutions. This is sometimes referred to as "Gold Shyness" and some of the symptoms, in order of severity, are:

• Unable to hold the sight on the gold through the shot.
• Unable to prevent release when on the gold or when the clicker drops.
• Unable to get the sight near the gold.
• Unable to achieve full draw.

Occasionally, an archer will go through these stages as the symptoms become worse. And of course, the knowledge that there is a problem only increases the fear and uncertainty. Target panic is a psychological problem which stems from a lack of confidence and is a very real problem for many archers.

There are several approaches to overcoming this problem, depending on the individual:

• Go back to basics. Pick up a beginner's bow, some old arrows, stand near a blank boss with no target face on it and simply shoot arrows.
• Shoot with eyes closed (with care). Stand close to the boss, close your eyes and simply draw the bow. Opening your eyes for the first couple of shots is a good idea to ensure that the position is right. Concentrate on the feel of the shot.
• When you're comfortable shooting with these two methods, add a sight and a full-size target to the boss and gradually, over a period of weeks, reduce the size of the face and the distance to the target.

• Get a Formaster and use that when shooting at the target. This will improve confidence.

There are other issues that an archer may experience which could be due either a fault with the equipment or some fine tuning is required. It is important to maintain and keep your equipment clean as eventually this will affect your equipment and shooting.

Tuning Equipment

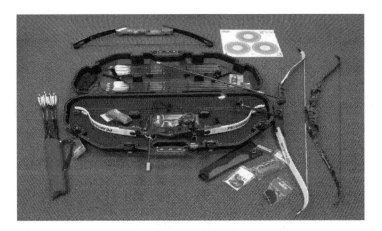

Tuning is the process of matching the archer, the arrow, the bow and the rest of the equipment (including the string, pressure button, etc.). It sounds like a complicated process, but in fact in its simplest form can simply be a case of shooting a couple of extra arrows each end and following the simple instructions below.

(34)

Tuning enhances accuracy in two ways:

- Helps to ensure that the arrow leaves the bow in the same way every time.
- Helps the archer by making the bow system more forgiving of poor technique and minor mistakes.

The bow should be tuned in five steps, and in the order below, otherwise you'll be tuning for ever more. Be aware, however, that you'll only ever be able to tune your bow as well as you can shoot it.

Prior to tuning, carry out the following checks:

- Ensure that the arrows are straight, properly fletched and have perfectly straight nocks.
- Ensure that the bow is set up as it would be for normal shooting, i.e. the correct bowstring, sight, stabilizers, rest, pressure button, etc.
- Ensure that the pressure button will not interfere with the fletching's (if so, rotate the nocks to ensure clearance).
- Set the center of the sight over the center of the shaft. Set the pressure button tension to a medium setting

1.Preliminary Setup

To start, the arrow must be close to the correct spine for the draw weight and style. An incorrectly spined arrow will be difficult, if not impossible, to tune (although a slightly stiff spine is easier to tune than one which is too weak). Refer to the spine chart for the supplier of the arrows. This is assuming, of course, that you know the draw weight of your bow. If not, ask someone to weigh it for you using a bowscale. If the arrow is incorrectly spined, then things can be done to change that situation, but these will be dealt with later.

2.Bracing Height

Get the bracing height right. Listen to the shot – does it sound good? Does it sound harsh? Set your bow at minimum bracing height and increase it steadily to maximum and listen to the bow (or better still, have someone else listen) as it is shot.

Go to a long distance where your groups are still nice and tight (e.g. 50m perhaps 70m) and start at the lower end of the manufacturers recommendation. Shoot some arrows (e.g. 18) and chart the vertical position of each arrow. Raise your brace-height slightly (e.g. 1/16 or 1/8 inch at a time) and again shoot some arrows. Also make a mental note of the noise the bow makes, or ask someone else, because you're too busy shooting and you shouldn't be paying attention to anything else but making one good shot (each time). Keep raising your brace-height until you are at the max. recommended brace-height. KEEP YOUR SIGHT ALWAYS THE SAME.

When you start at the lower end, the arrows hit somewhere on the target, raising the brace-height will probably make the arrows hit a bit higher than before, raising the brace-height a bit more will reduce the effectiveness of the bow, and the arrows will start to hit lower on the target.

3.Nocking Point

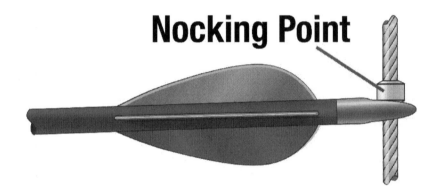

Set the correct nocking point height. If the nocking point is incorrect then the arrow will "porpoise", i.e. the point and tail of the arrow will oscillate in a vertical plane.

The nocking point can be checked as follows:

1. Paper tune. A frame is placed about 2 meters (6 feet) in front of the target. A sheet of paper is placed taunt over the frame. The archer then stands about 1 meter (3 feet) in front of the frame and shoots the arrows through the paper. From the direction of the tear in the paper, the nocking point can be adjusted.

2. Bare-shaft test. The theory behind bare-shaft tuning is that a bare shaft will continue in the direction it was shot since there are no fletching's to stabilize it, and will therefore give a true representation of any deviation from true. Shoot at least three fletched shafts and two identically aimed un-fletched shafts at a target of 15 to 20 yards. If the un-fletched shafts impact above the fletched shafts, the nocking point is too low., if the un-fletched shafts impact below the fletched shafts, the nocking point is too high (it is sometimes desirable to have the bare shaft impact just slightly below the fletched shafts to ensure that the nocking point is not too low as this could cause clearance problems.

4.Centre Shot

Centering the arrow is used to ensure that the "nodes" of the arrow leave the bow in direct alignment to the target. First, find the center of the bow limbs. To do this, place a piece of masking tape across the inside of each limb a few inches from the riser. Mark the center of each limb on the tape. Rest the bow by hanging it over the back of a chair, using the stabilizer/riser as a hook.

NOTE: it is important NOT to put any pressure on the limbs.

Nock an arrow and stand behind the bow, looking at the back of the riser. Looking through one eye and aligning the string with the marks on the masking tape, check the position of the arrow in relation to the string. If the arrow were central, then the arrow would align with the string, however, due to the bending motion imparted by a finger release, this is not desirable in such a setup.

Adjust the pressure button position until only the diameter of the arrow at the point is to the left of the bowstring (for right-handed shooters). Once this has been done, lock off the adjustment collar of the pressure button and leave it alone.

5.Arrow Spine

If the arrow spine is incorrect, then "fishtailing" will occur. I.e. the point and tail of the arrow will oscillate in a horizontal plane.

First, set the pressure button spring tension to a medium setting.

There are several ways to check for fishtailing, but by far the most reliable method is the bare-shaft test. Some archers use paper tuning but this method is more appropriate for compound archers and is highly unreliable for finger shooters as the arrow will leave with some side-side motion, and the paper tear will vary, depending on how far the archer is from the paper. Shoot at least three fletched shafts and two identically aimed un-fletched shafts at a target at 15 to 20 yards.

If the un-fletched shafts impact right (weak) of the fletched shafts, increase spring tension, decrease bow weight or decrease arrow point weight.

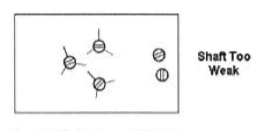

If the un-fletched shafts impacts left (stiff) of the fletched shafts, either decrease the pressure button spring tension, increase the bow weight or increase the arrow point weight.

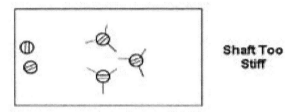

If you cannot get your bare shaft into the group then check for clearance, if the shaft is bouncing off the riser or something else, then it's never going to tune. Remember also to check your limb alignment. Remember that a button which is too soft may bottom-out (i.e. reach the limit of its travel), causing undesirable effects.

6.Clearance

Once the shaft is basically tuned, spray dry powder foot spray, dry deodorant or similar product onto the last quarter of the arrow shaft, fletching, arrow rest assembly and sight window near the arrow rest, then shoot the arrow (being careful not to disturb the powder). Check the powder for lines.

If there are clearance problems:

- Check if the arrow fletching is hitting the arrow rest, try rotating the arrow nock 1/32 of a turn. Continue rotating the nock until clearance is achieved
- Check that the arrow rest support arm does not protrude past the outside of the arrow shaft when the arrow is resting on the arm and is lying against the pressure button.
- Try lower profile fletching's or modifying your setup (stiffer/weaker arrows), different rest, etc.
- Move the pressure button slightly out from the bow, if all else fails.

7.Compensating for incorrect Spine

If you are shooting too weak a shaft, decrease draw weight, decrease the point weight, increase number of strands in the bowstring, decrease brace height. You might also try adding metal nocking points instead of dental floss.

If the shaft is too stiff, increase draw weight, increase the point weight, decrease number of strands in the bowstring, increase brace height.

Do not modify the point weight out with the acceptable balance point range (FOC or Front of Centre). Easton recommends the following ranges for target arrows:

Aluminum arrows: 7-9% ACCs   9-11% ACEs   11-16%

To calculate the FOC as a percentage, use the following calculation:
100 x (A-L/2) L, where A is distance from nock groove to balance point of finished arrow (including point, fletching's, etc.). and L is the shaft length (distance from nock groove to end of shaft).

Tiller Adjustment

The tiller is the name given to the balance of the limbs. Say, for example, you had a 38lb top limb and a 36lb bottom limb, then the bow would tend to tilt upward due to the excess load developed by the top limb, causing difficulty aiming. While the other tuning points mentioned above are focused on tuning the arrow to the archer, adjusting the tiller is more concerned with adjustment of the bow to the archer.

Modern bow limbs are usually manufactured as a matched pair, so why adjust the tiller? Simply because the riser and grip is not symmetrical. There are two adjustments which can be made to account for this:

Dynamic tiller - This is the force applied to the string by both limbs after release. Adjusted by tuning the nocking point

Static tiller - This is the force applied to the string by both limbs during the draw. Adjusted by changing the limb angle (by fitting shims or some other method). The recommended static tiller is usually somewhere between 1/8″ and 1/4″. This is measured by taking the distance from the limb (where the riser and limb meet) to the string (at right angles to the string). Typically, the bottom limb is 1/8″ closer to the string than the top limb. However, the way the archer holds the string and the bow will determine the actual position required for that archer.

To test static tiller, stand at 18m/20yds from the target (40/60cm), and put the sight on the target. Draw the bow slowly back to the anchor point. It is important that the hand moves directly to the anchor point, and that this is done slowly.

If the pin moves up, increase the tiller (increase lower limb poundage or decrease upper limb poundage). Similarly, if the pin moves down, decrease the tiller (decrease lower limb poundage or increase upper limb poundage).

CONCLUSION

The main areas of techniques have now been covered in addition to essential warm up, training, and common issues with perfecting that golden shot. It is worth noting that there is no "best technique" as we are all individuals and some methods will work better than others. Archery is never a case of "one glove fits all" and we will all have our own preferences and eventually develop our own, or alter current methods.

The importance of a good warm up cannot be underestimated therefore it is recommended that the exercises mentioned in chapter one is considered in addition to advice from your coach or club. Don't forget that you can practice your technique at home or work, with a friend, or in front of a mirror, and the training methods in chapter one will help you develop them muscles to perform on the range.

There is lot of actions that goes into making a shot, from positioning your feet, nocking the arrow, to releasing the shot, and perhaps a frustrating aspect of this is that the slightest error in any of these actions can ultimately affect your shot. This may put some people off but there would be no fun in the sport if it was easy, right?

If we hit gold every time it would not be long before we became bored and there would be little excitement. We should enjoy every shot, good and bad; laugh and learn from the bad shots and celebrate the good ones. Archery is a great sociable sport and the enjoyment comes in many forms, not just hitting gold.

If you are experiencing issues then hopefully chapter four has address these, however I always recommend talking to others at the club or even visiting a local archery supplier who are always happy to help.

As promised in the introduction, below is a glossary of archery terms for the budding beginners out there and finally, good luck on the range and enjoy yourself.

ARCHERY GLOSSERY

Arm-guard	Protective arm covering for bow-arm. Usually plastic, metal or leather.
Bare shaft	An arrow without fletching's
Barebow	A bow with no sight or aiming devices.
Berger Button	See Button
Bouncer (Bounce-out)	An arrow which strikes the target and then falls to the ground.
Boss	See Butt
Bow-scale	Device used to measure the draw-weight of a bow
Bow-square	Device used to measure bracing height and nocking-point position.
Bowyer	One who makes bows.
Brace Height	Distance between string and pivot–point of the bow (or pressure button).
Bracer	See Arm -guard.
Broadhead	Arrow point used in hunting. V-shaped with two or more cutting edges.
Butt	Backstop behind target face, usually straw or foam.
Button	Spring-loaded button. Used to absorb some of the sideways force of the arrow after release.
Cam	Eccentric pulley found on compound bows.

Chest-guard	Protective clothing used to prevent string catching on clothes or body.
Clicker	Metal or plastic device. Produces audible click when arrow is at full draw.
Clout	Archery competition where archers shoot at a peg in the ground.
Creep	Non-recoverable elongation unlike stretch which is basically elasticity or recoverable elongation
Crest	Colored markings on the arrow shaft
Compound Bow	Bow with eccentric pulleys and cables allowing high bow weights, but low weight at full-draw
Cushion Plunger	See Button.
Draw	Pulling the bowstring
Draw Length	The distance between the string and the pivot point at full draw
Draw Weight	Weight held by archer at full draw.
End	A specified number of arrows (usually 3, 4 or 6) shot between scoring
Face	Target – usually made from paper or card.
Field Archery	Archery shot in wooded course
Fish tailing	Movement of arrow from side to side during flight.

Fistmele	Archaic term referring to the Bracing height of the bow (which was often measured by using a fist with the thumb extended
FITA	Federation Internationale de Tir a L'Arc. International target archery federation.
Flemish Twist	The traditional longbow string with the loops made in the same manner as a rope, by twisting and splicing, rather than being a continuous strand of string material with the loops formed by serving. Can be used with recurves, but not recommended.
Fletching	The feathers or colored plastic "wings" attached towards the rear of an arrow.
Fletching Jig	Device used to hold arrow and fletching's to ensure consistent positioning while the glue is drying.
Flight Shooting	Archery shooting for maximum distance
Flu-flu	Large spiral fletching designed to slow arrow down quickly.
Foot marker	Device pushed into ground to ensure consistent foot position
F.O.C	Front of center – the balance point of the arrow when the point is fitted.
Gap Shooting	Using the distance between the arrow and the target as an

	elevation gauge.
Gold	Centre of the target (it is often colored yellow).
Gold Shyness / Gold fever	See Target Panic.
Grip	Where hand is placed on riser. Often plastic or wooden
Group	Several arrows shot close together.
Kisser Button	Small plastic device attached to the string for alignment with mouth at full draw
Lady Paramount	The lady in charge of an archery tournament. An honorary position only.
Limb	The energy-storing portion of the bow above and below the riser.
Longbow	Single-piece bow. Traditional archery.
Loop	Portion of the string which is strung around the limb tip.
Loose	The action of releasing the string.
Minnowing	High-speed movement of arrow from side to side during flight. (Indicative of poor clearance)
Nib	See Point.
Nock	Plastic device at the end of an arrow in which the string is placed
Nocking Point	Position on the string at which the nock is located.
Overdraw	Device used to permit archers to use arrows shorter than

	their normal draw length.
Paradox	A seemingly contradictory statement that may nonetheless be true. "Logic" dictates that a straight and balanced arrow must be shot straight at a target to hit it. The arrow must be aimed OFF of the target by a traditional archer in order to hit the target, due to the way the string reacts to the fingers on release.
Peak draw-weight	Maximum weight held by archer whilst drawing the bow
Pile	See Point.
Pivot-point	Position on grip farthest from the string.
Point	The pointed metal device inserted at the tip of the arrow.
Porpoising	Movement of arrow up and down during flight.
Pressure Button	See Button.
Puller	Rubber mat used to protect hands and provide grip when pulling arrows.
Recurve Bow	Bow with limbs which curve away from the archer.
Quiver	Pouch, usually worn around the waist or placed on the ground, used to hold arrows and other accessories.
Release	See Loose.
Rest	A wire or plastic device on which the arrow sits before

	and during the draw.
Riser	The handle of the bow.
Serving	Protective wrapping of string material around string to prevent wear
Shaft	The body of an arrow
Sight Window	See Window
Sling	Device to attach bow to archer's bow-hand.
Spine	The stiffness of the arrow shaft.
Stabilizer	Rod and weight combination attached to the bow to eliminate unwanted torque and vibration.
Stacking	Rapid increase in the draw weight of the bow, not in direct relation to the draw length
String Walking	Used by barebow archers. Fingers moved up and down string according to target distance.
Stringer	Device used to bend the limbs of a bow to allow the string to be attached.
Tab	Protector for string-fingers to prevent chafing.
Target Panic	Affliction where archer cannot hold the sight in the gold.
Toxophilite	Archer.
Tiller	A measure of the balance of the two limbs.
Tuning	Adjustment of the bow and arrow to provide most

	accurate and forgiving arrow flight
TFC	Torque Flight Compensator. Device used to absorb vibration
Vane	See fletching
Windage	Horizontal adjustment of a sight to compensate for wind-drift.
Window	Recessed area of riser above the grip.

Made in the USA
Monee, IL
23 September 2021